The Life and Art of Josan

The Life and Art of Josan

ALEX STEIN

WADE ROSEN PUBLISHING
BOULDER, COLORADO

Copyright © 2009 by Alex Stein

All rights reserved. No part of this work may be reproduced, except for the purpose of review, without written consent from Wade Rosen Publishing.

Published in the United States of America
Wade Rosen Publishing
PO Box 688
Boulder, CO 80306

information@waderosenpublishing.com

ISBN 978-0-9797746-0-7

10 9 8 7 6 5 4 3 2 1
First printing 2009

Design by Jane Raese

Printed in China

PREFACE

How it is done is immaterial. It is done! That ought to be enough for sense or for madness to obtain. To explain is like capturing birds. Where does one put them away, these explanations, when they are done? With the other words or flights?

Reasoning is not imagining! No bird is captured by clipping its wings.

> He is the river,
> who is fertile
> when flowing.
> He is the land,
> who stands
> in wait.
> To demand
> is to flower:
> that is growing!

—Josan
Boulder, CO
2007

Then, what? It all opens up again. The infinitely petaled realm

of the possible, with its infinitely petaled promises.

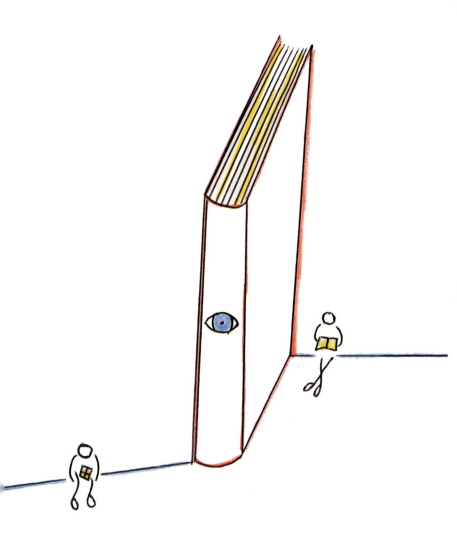

PART ONE
The Winged Part of Ourselves

Is the wind written on fallen leaves? Do we read with our feet when we walk? Do we read the earth?

It is possible
to climb too high—
or to fly too far—
  or to be too reasonable!

The days drifted by formlessly, like wards of a state mental institution.

If I start now, I can get there before the next tide...

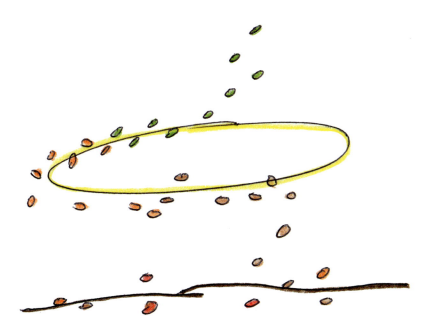

The leaves turn green,
the leaves turn brown,
the wind is the water
in which the leaves drown.

Peaches!
A moment before,
they were still
ripening!

Perhaps the gods have *not* ceased their dancing, after all.

"Aren't days strange?" she says. "All for not sleeping, perhaps, they continue to exist."

(What, then? After everyone is gone, the sun will no longer rise or set? Well, would you? Could you? In that circumstance? Under those —brr!— conditions?)

Hold light,
butterfly—
for a short
life, praise!

Swans Upon the Lake!

The slate/upon which figures swim! Ye gods! Are ye really former professors of metaphysics?

A Mermaid!

The song of the mermaid has an especial attraction for one particular type of sailor. I mean that one who does not seek the land, but rather for the deeper water. As for myself, knowing only what I know, I pray to God not to die in the arms of a poet.

This desert soul, so painstakingly cultivated, whereupon the slightest touch leaves so definite an impression. Is it really an order of mystic abeyance? Or merely of Eros, a final temptation?

In the life you may be poised on the threshold, while in the art you have already achieved the chamber.

Moon/rose!

A thousand years/between cockcrows!
Cast no shadow!
Leave no bones!

It is not that the snail flies. Ah, but that time passes...

Rain that has
some other place to go—
falls on my roof
and rushes in a fury
from my gutter.

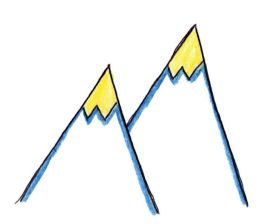

What should I do with this bubble of happiness? This bubble of happiness that is swelling inside my chest? Shall I call it profound? Shall I call it transcendence? When it is nothing more than a birthright? Available to all who are human and searching and guided by conscience.

(You and I shall love one another until all is returned to the sand grains and dust from which it first arose: the belly of it all—to be fed again, from bodiless Being, through the divine, originary umbilicus.)

The will that drives the body comes through the spirit—

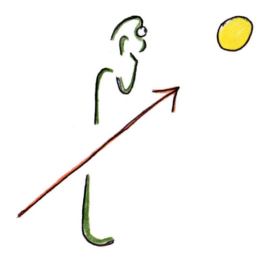

Thus it is—though rare—that one can, with experience, become more innocent.

(Oh, you scoffers! Suppose that for "innocent," I had substituted the word "holy?" What then? Could you still not believe?)

It would be funny, with all the ships crossing continuously upon that ocean, if you could not buy a berth for love nor money.

Funny like the fury at the base of despair. Funny like the solace of faith in the absence of the miracle. Funny like a shadow that lives more fully than does the creature from which it falls.

The ghost ship to end all dreams has finally arrived, my dear.

You do have a harbor, don't you?

"I ... I wrote a book, you know ..."

"Yes ... yes ... and I'm sure it was a very good book."

"It was ... it was very good ... it was."

There is something sanguine about the sight of small boats at anchor, rocking in a close harbor.

(Sails furled ... like you or I, rolled to rest, after a blown out passion.)

Imagine, my friend, you
have been sleeping so soundly,
that not even the
dinning bell,
twice daily
overhead, has
been enough
to awaken
you.

You have thought all along—wherever you are!—perhaps that you are too good for that place,

certainly that you do not fit. But of course you do fit. You must! How else could you have become embedded?

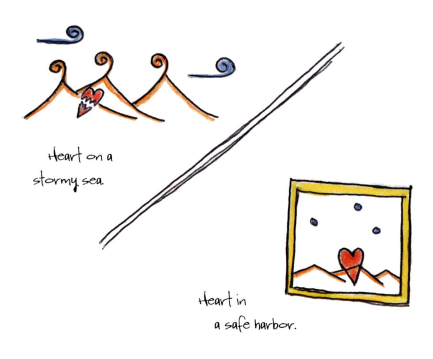

Heart on a stormy sea.

Heart in a safe harbor.

Artist on a windswept plain, under the star of faith.

Psyche's (two golden butterflies) endlessly inventive!

It is not the harness against which the horse bridles, but the absence of wings—it is not, that is, the captivity of the body, but the ambition of the mind.

At some point, I simply recognized that certain expressions

of my understanding were profound. From there to artistry, it was (only!) a question of perfect discrimination.

It would be a strange life, indeed (even, perhaps, beyond bearing),

if our destiny and our desire had no point of coincidence.

Is this my Odyssey? Is this my Odyssey? Round and round the same little island of ghosts? Tumbling to the same sirens?

A lost professor in search of his inamorata?

I do not know about honor—I only know about art—but you may rest assured that if The Dragon should ask me to get

down on my hands and knees and lick scum from the lip of a fetid puddle, I would know at once that this was not The Dragon. I honor nothing that does not seem to honor itself.

The sun's a mirror of eternity, in that one may not stare directly into it, without going blind.

(Which is how the poets can reconcile both irony and faith within themselves.)
(Or, rather, why they must!)

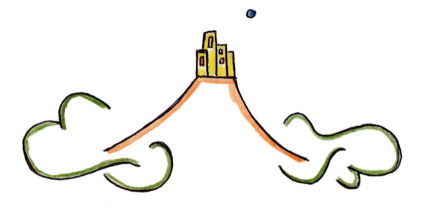

What is the world? Some say that it is a big university, a big sprawling campus whereon we scurry like students from one incomprehensible class to another, desperately hoping to encounter a professor not whom we understand, but who understands us—our private, individual concerns and needs, the unique terms (if you will) by which we might provoke the true ceremony of our commencement.

Am I then beyond the brute force, the redemptive power, of love?

Thrown back upon the cold solace of mind?

Imagine, if she flew right into my arms—how should I carry

her more gently than the breath that blew her to me?

I am thinking, as she speaks with me, of butterflies and of water—of Psyche and of the elemental state of Being itself. Of the many misfortunes that can befall us imaginative people,

and of the misfortune it sometimes seems to be to have attained to the condition of consciousness at all.

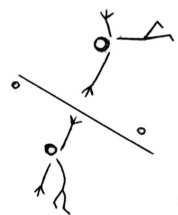

(... that desire which is the immortal part of us ... the remnants, here on Earth, of the divine ...)

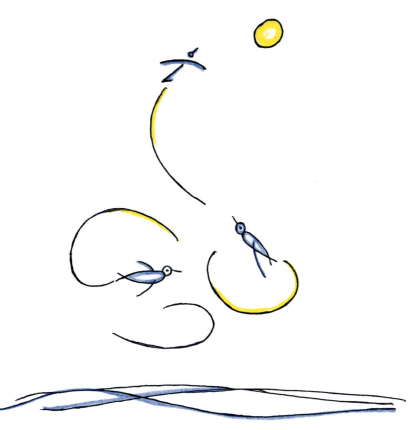

My feeling is that one person is no more dead than the next. We are all just dead people along a contiguous, radiant spectrum. Some of us falling into the range of the visible, and some of us falling into the range of the invisible. As with, say, the unborn dead in the ultra-violet, and the afterlife dead in the infra-red. While the dead so-called "the living" occupy the median.

One might ask oneself if there is any relevance to this line of thinking. No, there is not. Nor is there any such condition as relevance. Neither is there, between the corporeal and the incorporeal, any sort of schism.

(Meanwhile, as the critics might put it, back on planet Earth, there are innumerable diversions.)

You get used to letting fate sweep you along, to taking no hand in your own destiny, even though you have these strong, certain premonitions. Then one day you awaken—still here!—while the one for whom you have been longing awaits—on the other side of the world!

(Is this then, you ask yourself, for the hundredth—no, the hundred thousandth—time, what poetry is supposed to solace?)

Instinct!

Habitable planet, yes?

Church and dragon!

To have nests

in two worlds,

and never be done
with leaving ...

Ah, that is no life,
but a poet's.

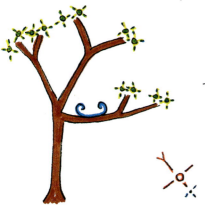

Oh! You thought it was the raft upon which you would be crossing.

Ho, no! When the time comes for you to cross, The Dragon will take you himself, upon his back!

My life is steady and predictable. It's like Flaubert said: "Be bourgeois in your life that you may be vain and inflammatory in your art." That was after he meditated atop the Great Pyramid.

I am aware that the resources of our planet are finite, and while I believe that the resources of the mind are infinite, I do not pretend to believe that solutions to all our problems lay therein.

(Though one might, perhaps, imagine the infinite mind of the planet itself.)

Time, by constraining space, gives rise to the energy of form. If we had eternity in an instant, the "nothing" (out of which the sages say the "something" arises) would simply persist.

Perhaps the fish that I seek is not even in this pond into which (year after year) I have cast my lure.

"What?" you may ask. "Not in this pond? Impossible! Not to speak of the fact that there are no other ponds. You are simply not fishing, my friend, with enough conviction! Or, perhaps, it may be that you are not so pure of heart as you believe yourself to be."

(As if it were a question of faith, and not of sheer phenomenological immutability.)

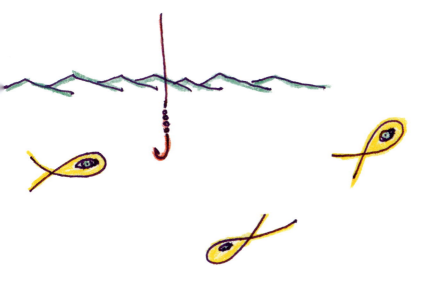

Self-portrait of the artist (as he would have it done by another) crying "More light! More light!"

Here is the church where—under the ceremony of union is consecrated—ah, in fact no priest ever drew true breath who had not,

first, gills and second, affairs of his own, suspended.

The ruined church? The resurrection!

Ah, Josan—
you're heaven's body, now!

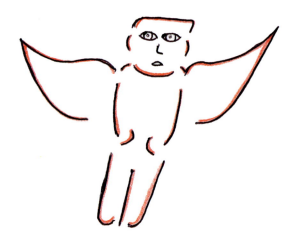

To enter into the very fundament of creative activity—
(which is light's body)—is to enter into the winged part
of ourselves.

It is as important to dwell in one's house
as it is to ride upon dragons.

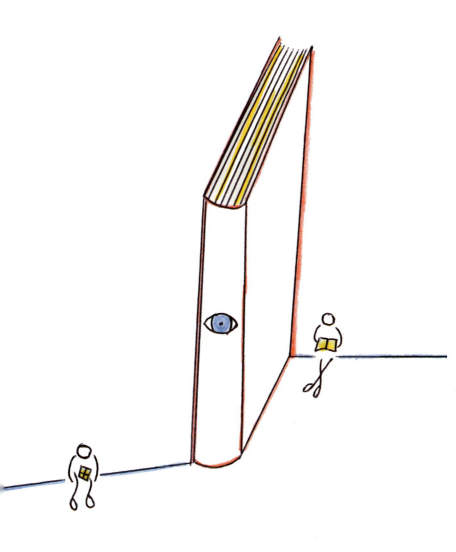

PART TWO

The Field Unfurrowed

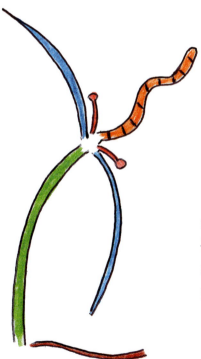

Like a tiger
that has sprung
from a lily—
I am of two minds.

An unexpected guest, at an inconvenient hour, eh kiddo?

And with what ardency, knocking!

what if the spirit of romance were not (every so often) to boil back into my system? would that mean that I had achieved some high plateau? or merely that the daily neurosis of living had blown me (at last) too cold to feel the little spring flowers of hope opening themselves innocently toward me.

When you are in love (and you elders might want to close your eyes and hearken back) the entire world is, from the inside out, illuminated. Young lovers walking along the garbage strewn streets of the East Village might be walking along the pearl strewn beaches of the Indian Ocean.

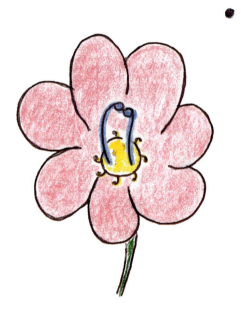

All I know about happiness, alas!, is that it is born of fusion.

Flesh is the wood that we throw upon the fire that is our workaday sexual desire. The burgeoning light which

results—our exaltation—is merely the fleeting chemical condition of a corrupted element.

(But how sad to think of it like that, eh? And how insulting to the art of human relationship.)

"Boys are so shy," she says, which is true, but girls ... they are just so ... transparent ...

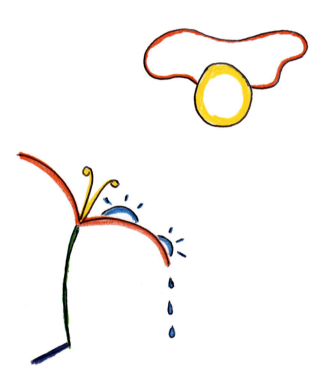

(Like rainwater on the petal of a blossom.)

Tomorrow ... today ... what

does it matter? You and I live together already, untroubled, on a distant sea.

Art's funny, 'cause if you can't sell it, you probably can't give it away.

(Or, you can, but like a Down's Syndrome kid might give a macaroni sculpture to his social worker.)

Upon the flowers,
in the dawn—
the memory of stars,
in dew.

The world is like a crystal of sugar that, stirred into the mind,

dissolves. Nothing is other than we have—either collectively or individually—willed it to be. Nothing will ever change, save as we change ourselves. This is what is meant by "the power of love over death."

You, my friend (yourself, alone ...)

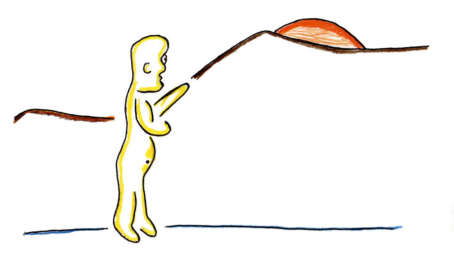

are the light of the world!

Woman on a Horse!

Once there was a woman who loved to ride.

Ah, it would be imprudent to make more of this than it is.

Every flower that blooms—little by little it opens, until it is completely open.

The woman must not dismount at this village, nor at the next.

Oh, nor at the next either.

You men would do well to pay attention, as if this were a parable.

Pirate Maiden!

Once there was a maiden who was abducted by pirates and held prisoner aboard their ship for many years.

She grew to like the life and became a pirate herself, with a tri-corner hat and a silver dagger.

She plundered and she pillaged and she, too, abducted maidens.

"Yargh!" growled the other pirates. "You are a fine mate!"

But, who knows what she might have been had she not been abducted. Are you or I any less creatures of chance? Determining within the box of our prospect the measure of our will?

Even the monkey must learn
his way around the tree ...

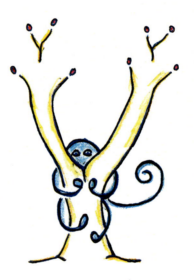

So you and I, our star-
dreams failures, will climb the
next time (higher) with that
much more agility.

You have
broken my
heart.

Almost, it
seems, again,
for the first
time ...

Now what? Wave after wave of happiness? Is it ridiculous to be so content with the resolution of a conflict in which the only part you took

was to stand fast in your confusion?

The dream fire will burn itself out, no matter how much dream tinder is heaped upon it. And all the dream boys and dream girls who flew from

it like sparks, must fall again like ashes.

As if I had
not understood
what dreaming was
before you
awakened me ...

If you look up, you
will see the receding galaxy,
into the gravitational pull of
which you are being sucked, inexorably.
(On the other hand, it is always best—
at any height—not to look down.)

I ask her, offhand, if she has any mental disorders—"depression," she replies, even-toned, which for some reason makes my heart leap.

(Once upon a time, in another world, another woman, in response to a similar question, simply pulled her shirt off over her head.)

Spilled wine, or wine still in the glass.
Poem on the page, or poem still in the ink.

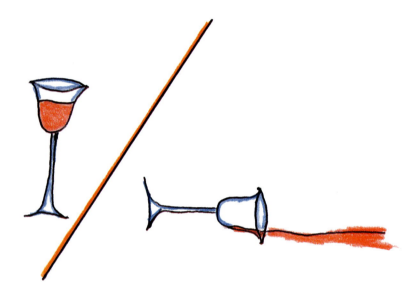

(Consummation, the old wise say, is a dissipate.)

There are
giants, of
course, and
then there
are those
who merely
have their
heads
in the clouds.

The struggle that goes on all night to
remove from my heart the knife with which
you have impaled me
I deem honorable.
Such a wound as
one can take to
bring life out of the shadows ... reveals much
about the erotic nature of animosity.

Corpulent Coleridge, in-
vited to dine
with virgins on teacakes pre-
ferred ghosts and wine.

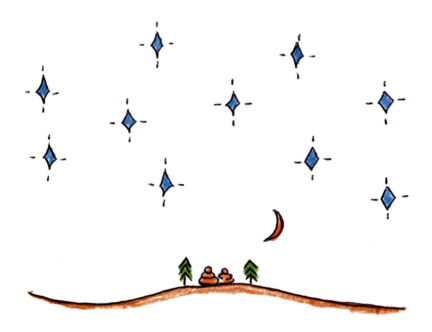

The sky on this autumn night
is like an apple tree—
lacking not even a ladder.

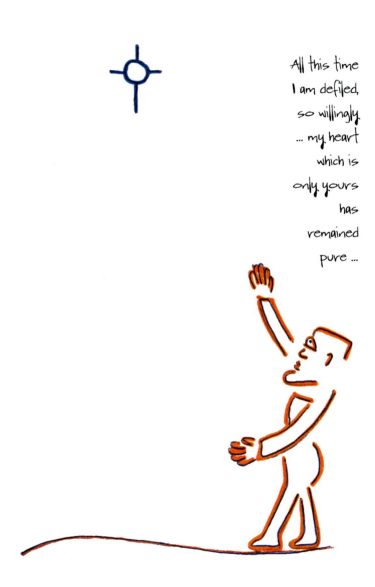

A Portrait of Fyodor

You have to ask yourself (but casually) if any one person can add a single iota to the sum of your personal (possible) happiness.

The human equation: $u + i = ?$

You'd need a team of clairvoyant Princeton Einsteins and about a hundred million chalk boards to even begin to answer that one.

The woods are lonely—with you over there and me over here—

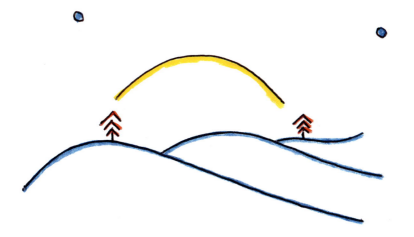

(Did you desire me, though, as I do you, that would build a bridge between us—upon which it would be nothing to cross over.)

An Artist!

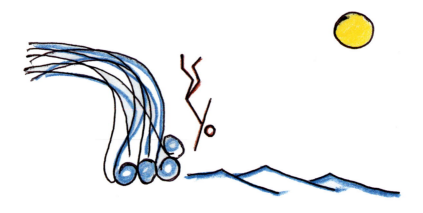

Narcissism, delusion ... these are the straits into which an artist might tumble ...

(Self-pity, mendacity ... scholarship!)

Thereafter—which will recur that love of simplicity upon which rock his church was first set.

Poetry is like the beam from a lighthouse, shining upon the watery grave where the poet last went under.

The question of immortality is like the question of whether or not one can breathe an entire cosmos into one's lungs in the course of an hour, and exhale that cosmos out steadily through the millenniums that follow.

These bodies are the mendicants that time sows through space ...

(Even a king's castle is a small coin in a vast cosmic realm of exchanges.)

Immortality? That's—I think—a long way off!

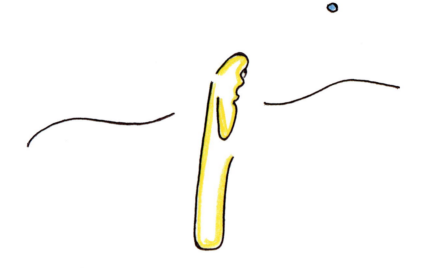

(Although the prospect of relentless materiality, which the scientists seem to be holding out as some sort of a promise, strikes me as more in the nature of "an extended sentence," than the "governor's pardon" it supposes itself to be.)

Eros and Psyche (their union sanctified by its own delight) were wed in the chapel of spring, before a congregation of every blown blossom since time immemorial.

(What mumbo-jumbo, then, of Catechism, shall you and I await?)

The mind
is a flower—
inside which
the seas
and the skies
of tomorrow
are forming!

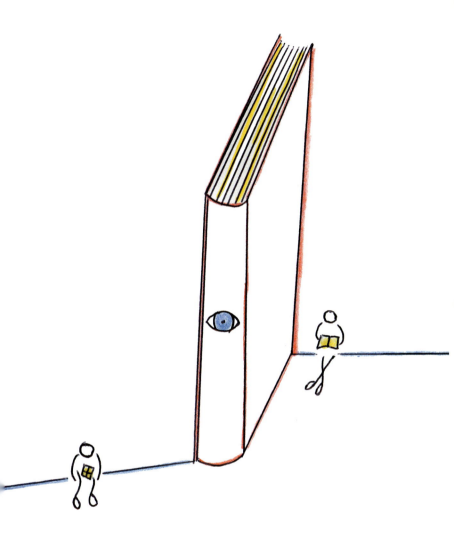

PART THREE
The Troll to whom the Scroll Refers

Once there was a troll who had lived for forty years in a cave in the desert.

For forty years he had done nothing but eat bugs and read and reread the scroll that he had found in the cave upon his arrival.

The scroll said, "A troll will live in this cave for forty years, at the end of which time an angel will appear before him bearing great tidings."

It was the morning of the fortieth anniversary of his arrival in the cave. He stepped outside and waited.

The sun rose. A scorpion scurried by. The sun fell.

After all, the troll thought, an angel is not a train to come on a schedule. He went back into his cave to sleep.

And after all, he thought, awakening suddenly in the middle of the night, it may be that the troll to whom the scroll refers is a different troll entirely.

Then, even the desert slept.

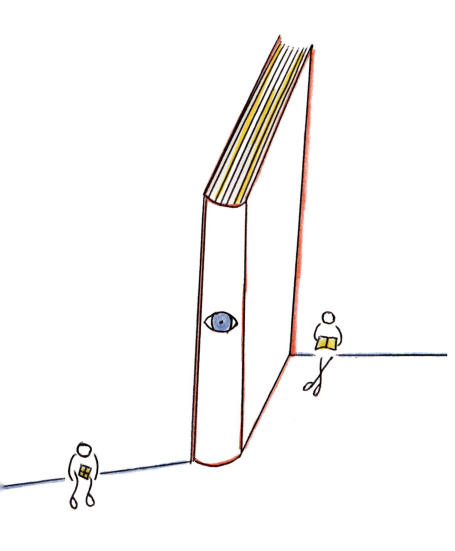

PART FOUR

I Am of Two Minds

The devil does not blink, even once, the while that god's gaze is averted.

(How then do we—any of us—enter at those good, gold gates?)

It's funny to think that a few words stand between the possibility and the realization.

   (But what those words are, my dear, and to whom they ought to be spoken, these are the maddening imponderables. Hunger! Thirst! Are they the shadows? Or are they, in truth, the bread?)

Stood on the beach this morning, looking at the ocean. No revelations, but we are insignificant, I'll grant you that. One drop of water, followed by another, followed by another.

Eon piled atop eon, piled atop eon. Finally, the palm of one's own hand seems beyond comprehension.

"After a certain point," says Da Buddha, "there is no slowing down. The wheel spins faster, and then faster still. Time and space condense. Everything can be held like a pebble in the palm of the

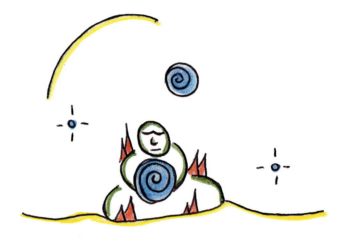

hand and yet nothing can be seized. We are motionless, weightless. Unborn and unmade. We have not even a name—that one thing we have thought confidently to call ourselves by."

A few steps to the left and I would be (as they say in Spiritville) on a different ledge entirely.

(Still, however, precipitous.)

Your soul? Pfth!!
Sooner guard your
crown, my friend,
your garden, and
your robe...

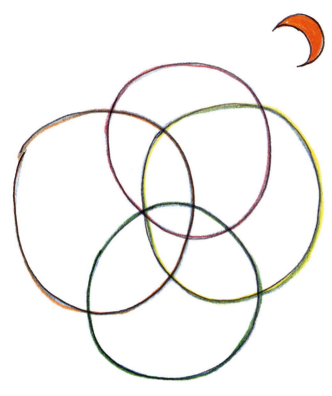

All the worlds
are
interwoven.
You and I
enmeshed,
under how
many
moons?

The sense, in viewing a painting by Van Gogh, that one is looking directly into the eye of the painter himself—

And his works that seem to say, "I would rather than genius have had peace of mind, wouldn't you?"

That nightmare's/just sea foam!

Same old horse/and plow.

Just the harrow/of a different field.

The Pearl!

The sky is an oyster, oh, yes! And the stars are like grains of sand. And a pearl is in the oyster.

Look! The mind is an oyster and ideas are like grains of sand and a god is in the oyster.

There are no miracles, there are only fathomless seas, out of which you and I come like stones of fire ... unreachably inside ourselves.

Who are the gods, anyway, and what have they prepared us for? A.D. 2004! Still the Greeks and the Romans. Still, somehow, the Laodicians, the Trojans, the Babylonians. Still the ancient civilizations returned in us to wonder.

Mr. and
 Mrs. Blake

"I have returned from Paradise. You were there," Mr. Blake says. "You were wearing much less."

"Ah, yes," Mrs. Blake replies. "In your heaven, I would be."

An Ox!

Plowing the sea/the field's unfurrowed!

Our deeds are nothing, we ourselves are nothing.
Good and evil are like sparks that fall in a pool.
And yet ... and yet ...
Had you only married me, I might have found some way of changing all that.

You and I, drunk on communion wine.

The bride and the groom of Christ ... wrapped up in wings of fire.

Self-portrait of the artist as a bucket of water, burning, with a fish in it.

When the stage is properly set, she will sing an aria! Meanwhile, the fruits from the highest branches do not elude her.

Perhaps no larger than the reflection of myself in your undilated pupil—as small as small can be.

In the reflecting pool/arrow and quiver.

You who think that there are limits to everything and that there are rules: you create the limits, you impose the rules.

Together we might be all one mind divining a single over-riding need. The world might be a unified field, but a single strand, as well, in some spider-god's miraculous web.

The groom?

Sure, he is worth nothing to you or me, but you see the bride will climb the tower just to reach his room ... her veil torn away ... her gown in tatters.

An impregnable fortress! Ah, yes, perhaps—but hardly an enviable solitude.

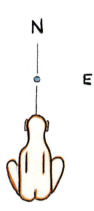

 If thought is put into an object, if an idea is given form, then can it be said that that object, that form, possesses consciousness? And, if so, what is the nature of that consciousness? (What, in general, is consciousness? Is it self-awareness? Could one define consciousness as an ability? And, if so, what is the nature of that ability? In a person, we might say it is the capacity to project imaginatively through time and space. But in a block of stone? In a clump of clay?)
 If the physical arose from an idea and if that consciousness is a parcel of that form, is that consciousness still animate? Must we insist that it died into its reckoning?

"There is within each of us an eternal, devouring flame—within which is set a continuous, eternal throne—upon which sit a succession of selves—each of whom is, in his or her own right, eternal—each of whom is, in his or her own right, ephemeral," says Da Buddha. "A star is not longer in the instance of its burning than we ourselves are."

(Anyhoo, that's the shtick he taps to at the Bodhi-Pavillion, in the Nirvana district of downtown Buddhaville.)

 A list of the secret ingredients.

A flood (while not exactly frogs or locusts) would certainly cast some doubt upon our moral status as a citizenry. Ah, the common weal!

The grandeur of events must thrust it upon us that we do not live entirely in the theatre of our own sensibilities.

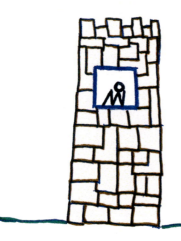

God, forgive me, but why are they all so stupid? Is it the behest of my muse to keep me lonely

that makes them seem so, or are they really just monkeys with stones?

The mistakes he makes are the mistakes of someone so hotly engaged in the world, that he cannot afford (has not the time to take) a moment's reflection.

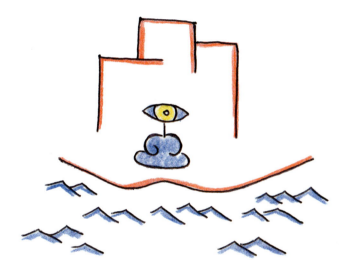

(Unlike my mistakes which are the awful result of speculating upon imaginary futures—as if there existed only my will, alone in the vacuum of space.)

"You have a gift for the world," says Da Buddha. "I do?" asks the supplicant.

"No," replies Da Buddha, "I mean your idiot double. Of course you do."

Well, and what is it? The nature of this "gift." Of what does it consist?

"Your terror over the possibility of its inexpressibility," replies Da Buddha, wittily.

Well, and define "its," from the preceding assertion, please.

"Its?" says Da Buddha. "Its is this: doubt as prayer; the paradox of doubt; doubt as faith."

"That's my gift for the world?" asks the supplicant.

"Sure," replies Da Buddha. "Why not?"

—"Where can a fellow go 'round these parts to find love?" asks the cowboy.

—"Well, I guess that would be our saloon," replies a local. "You don't got anything against whores, do you?" He adds.

—"No," replies the cowboy. "I guess I don't. It's only a nomenclature anyhow, ain't it?"

—"Why I guess it is, at that," the local replies, happily (surprised, as any of us would be—Old West or New—to find himself involved in a calm and reasonable exchange of views).

The devil is chance, that is all—

playing havoc against hope and prayer—both!
(God, too, is the law of probability on a miraculous run.)

O, after all, who are we to one another,
who are not even fully known to ourselves?
Ah, my child, we are questions in bones,
thrown out from rivers of light.

—"The train's a'comin'!"
—"Oh, yeah? About when's it due?"
—"Should be here any minute."

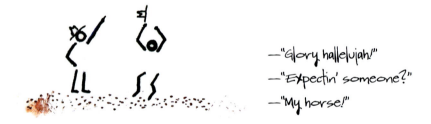

—"Glory hallelujah!"
—"Expectin' someone?"
—"My horse!"

(Some arrows fly farther than others...)

Easter Sunday is what? The Resurrection?
Oh, yeah. I got my own reasons for internalizing that archetype.

Religions are based on more or less coherent systems of symbols. Symbols are external images that seem to have their roots in the buried reaches of the psyche. That is what is meant when it is said that "deep calls to deep."

The priest who would intercede, invariably obfuscates.

That is because so many priests who believe they have the divine calling are actually in fealty to what Freud would call the Super-Ego.

Portrait of Fyodor as the spurned lover.

My proof of a higher power is in the genius of certain artists. That is (to state it clearly) in the genius, not in the artist.

Careful, sir, if you want to

pluck the petal whole, to tug first, gently, on the root.

For a while, you and I were married, were we not?

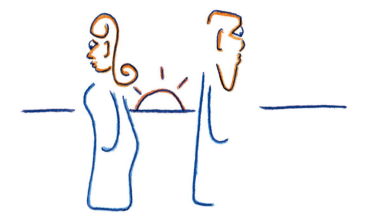

I mean, in another world.

"No matter where you think you have arrived," says Da Buddha, "go back to the beginning. Start over again. Refresh your ignorance, your innocence, your awe. Even your virginity, if you can steal it away from the house of ill-fame in which it has been languishing since you sold it off."

How can anyone know what part of it is love, and what that other creature of the deep— possession!

Perhaps there is
a seed somewhere
you have put to sleep.
Ye autumn winds!
Blow and whisper.

Dew had condensed
on the tongue of the bell
that rang this morning.

The gods of art
who protect me ...

realize why you
do not understand.

"It is fortunate for you that you struck a chord in me, my little pitiable one, otherwise you'd have no part of art at all."

"Oh, thank you, sir, and please, may I be punished more?"

"Ah, yes, you certainly may ... this time for your goodness, or for your innocence?"

There are seas within us—or, let us say, rather, bodies of energy possessing the primal ebb and scope and flow of those bodies which—when we apprehend them sensually—we call "seas."

When Christ "calmed the waters" and "walked" upon them, this is—fundamentally and for starters—all that was meant.

(Which is not to preclude the miraculous, the literal "chapter and verse" possibility of His mastery over the elements—much less to imply that the biblical narrative is mere metaphor.) In fact, the pure, perceptible, physical act may be simply the logical extension of the abilities arising from such disciplined attainment as the more readily conceivable aforesaid.)

(Potatoes are to creatures of madness, what stars are to

creatures of grace: (the habitual mirror of their paradigm.)

You would be surprised at what is possible, my dear...

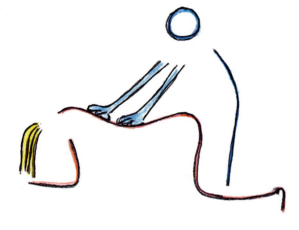

in ordinary lives.

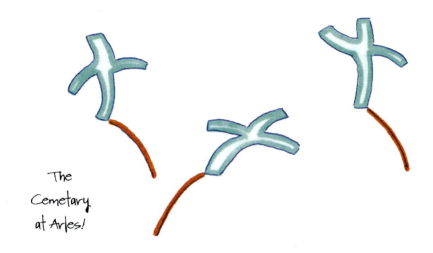

The Cemetary at Arles!

Undo life!/For the love of Christ!

Or live/like a shadow/in glory.

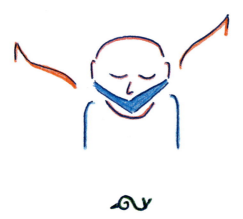

ABOUT THE AUTHOR

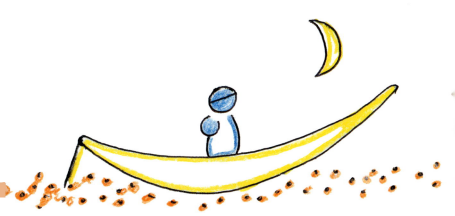

    Josan is an artist and a story-teller who has traveled all around the country in a boat to prove that there is always enough water available for those who truly want to float.

    He crossed the desert one moonlit night, as if on a sail through the ocean. "Calm seas," was his only comment upon that miracle.

WWW.WADEROSENPUBLISHING.COM

WWW.ALEXSTEINWORKS.COM